# Plant Songs

SELECTED BOOKS BY JAMIE K. REASER

*Dawn Songs:*
*A Birdwatcher's Field Guide to the Poetics of Migration*

*Truth & Beauty:*
*Poems on the Nature of Our Humanity*

*RidgeLines:*
*A View of Nature and Human Nature*

*Conversations with Mary:*
*Words of Attention and Devotion*

*Coming Home:*
*Learning to Actively Love this World*

# PLANT SONGS

## NEW & SELECTED POEMS

JAMIE K. REASER

TALKING WATERS PRESS · *Schuyler, Virginia*

Copyright © 2024 Jamie K. Reaser/Talking Waters Press

All Rights Reserved. This book may not be reproduced, stored in a retrieval system, or transmitted in any form or by any means without permission from the publisher, except as a purchased product conveyed in electronic format.

Individual works may be shared for presentation and discourse in any format, providing that the author and book are fully credited as follows:

Reproduction of these works for commercial use or nonprofit fundraising is prohibited without permission of the publisher/author.

ISBN: 978-0-9968519-6-1
First Edition 2024
Talking Waters Press
Schuyler, Virginia
Cover images: Jamie K. Reaser
Author photo: Meredith McKnown Photography

*Our physical living is held together by plant sacrifice.
We eat, wear, and are sheltered by plants and plant material.
Nearly all of our medicines are plant-derived.
We need to take time with them, get to know them.*

– JOY HARJO, from *Poet Warrior*

# Contents

**SPRING**

3   Botanical
5   Daffodil
6   Do Branches Delight?
7   Epigeal Ephemeral
8   Gifting You Roses
10   Imbolc
11   It's a Dandelion
12   Madre De La Selva
13   The Blue Iris
14   The Crocus
15   The Dogwood
16   The Garden Iris
17   The Last Day
18   The Redbud (Pleasure)
19   The Rhododendron
21   The Unfurling
22   The Way a Flower Opens
23   The Fiddlehead Song
26   What We Want from a Flower

**SUMMER**

29   A Hot Summer
31   A Summer Moment
32   Before Falling was a Fear
34   Berries
35   Berry Picking
36   Bloom

- 38  Grape
- 39  Lavendar
- 40  Lilies
- 42  Listening To Trees
- 43  Nectar
- 44  Queen Anne's Lace
- 45  Spiderwort
- 47  The First Strawberries
- 50  The Flowers
- 52  The Primary Drought
- 54  The Trees Speak
- 55  The Fire Song
- 58  When Men Sell Their Souls

### AUTUMN

- 61  Acorns
- 62  And the Oak
- 64  Asters (Identity Matters)
- 66  Asters Under a Hunter's Moon
- 67  Bittersweet
- 68  Blue Lobelia
- 69  Fallen
- 70  Ginseng Thieves
- 71  Goldfinches On Sunflower
- 72  Leaving
- 73  Pawpaws
- 74  The Annual
- 76  The Cattail
- 77  The Names of Trees
- 78  Then, Nothing
- 79  The Wedding Flower
- 80  To Tell the Truth About Persimmons

- 81 Until, Then
- 82 When Dreams Dry Up

**WINTER**
- 87 Below the Crisp-Capped Snow
- 88 Fallow
- 91 In the Belly
- 93 Leaves Rising
- 95 One Winter
- 96 Plants In Winter In Six Versus
- 98 Pruning
- 99 Roses Are Out of Season
- 101 The Ancestral Tree
- 102 The Berries
- 103 The Black Walnut Tree
- 105 The Roots
- 111 The Winter Woods
- 112 The Seed
- 114 White Pines
- 116 Winter Berry
- 117 Winter Branches
- 118 Wonderland
- 119 Yule

- 121 *Acknowledgements*
- 123 *About the Author*

# Spring

# Botanical

The human animal
is plant derived:
from field to table,
nourishment for the soul
when strolling the garden
or turned wild again
in the dark wood
along the ferned stream,
and in companionship
for those who can still hear
the plant songs sung
to the morning dew
and whipping winds,
to accompany the birds,
and just because
there is reason enough to sing.
The artists, the composers:
how they have been enchanted
by the plant spirits
and we remain so in their works,
time being no rival for passion.
What on Earth?
Every breath made possible.
Every sentiment a flower.
And yet, we cut it all away:
usefulness and tidiness
and statements about
our worth.

Every dusty botanical specimen
in a museum drawer
is prepared to say something
about our humanity.

# Daffodil

His yellow smock
offers no apologies
for its brazen attempt
to embody the bold cry
that we fear might pass
our own lips.

Even in culturally accepted
moments of
ecstatic inspiration –

Such as the viewing
of spring-time blooms –

So many will remain
wanton of their
expression
of glory.

# Do Branches Delight?

Do branches delight in the bird? Do they hold tight to the nest, feeling proud and responsible? Do they believe the singing is for them – a lyrical prayer for a long life, or maybe a blessing as gratitude – reciprocity? Is it coincidence that their leaves come and go as the birds come and go?

Do birds delight in the watcher? Do they feel seen in the way that humans long to be seen? Do they take note of form and behavior – field characteristics? Do they want our affections, or are mornings for them about the fullest extent of their tolerance – for some short, for others long? Are we to be unrequited lovers? Oh, my dearest, no – I have reason to believe that we keep rising early and showing up in edgy places because we've had the experience of something looking into our eyes and choosing to stay for a while. Choosing our company. Choosing us.

I go to the woodland, the meadow, and the water's edge with hopes and dreams, with just enough knowledge to pry the magic loose from the breaking day. When I lift the binoculars, it can be science and it can be mythos – simultaneously. Don't take one with you unless you bring the other. It's a rose-breasted grosbeak and it's a god whose heart bleeds, his lament for the soul of man too great to be contained within his feathered chest.

In the branches, there is song.

# Epigeal Ephemeral

Epigeal: adjective of botanical nature.
Growing on or close to the ground.
Grounded. Grounded, yet emerging.
A well-rooted aspiration to be a
bold-something despite the vulnerabilities
inherent in just showing up.

*Hepatica nobilis*, a docile woodland
plant of buttercup relation and oak
familiarity, roots in calcareous, clay-rich
soils, emerges in late winter or early
spring to call me out into the world again.
Her liver-leaf, hairy stem, and purple
petals are my body's unfolding and
the beauty that I want to put onto this
Earth, somehow.

To be there, intentionally visible, just to
the other side of the dark season requires
something that little plants have mastered
and humans are still apprenticing to. We
are learning, I hope, to find our way back
to well-lit places with a vigorous resilience.
I'll call it wisdom.

The offerings of flowers and a generous self should never be squandered. This world can't wait for reluctant witnesses.

Love is here.

And, then, gone.

# Gifting You Roses

I have twelve in my hand, yellow and tight.
On long stems, green and wildly thorned.
I have captured the sun
and cast the warm glow of its light on memories
and truths and tomorrows.
Gratitude might be the answer to all of our questions.
I am grateful.
Do you know this day?
Do you know it, truly?
We cannot repeat miracles. What arrives,
arrives only once.
Do you see these petals?
Each is a never again, and I'm thankful for the opportunity
to trace the silken thread of their veins.
How can we not but look upon each as a miracle?
Yes, gratitude must be the answer to all our questions.
Today I have put my nose against
the windowpane aside your front door.
I am carrying twelve yellow roses
because.
Yes,

because.

# Imbolc

The pendulant snowdrops
are here, hosting the sweet morning light.
It's time to rise and call in the dragons.
There's much yet to be undone
to make way for what is yet to arrive
when the dried oak leaves are pushed aside
by the blades of the most daring of daffodils,
when the pond's still waters once again
quake with the intersecting ripples loosed
by the undulating throats of calling frogs,
when our bodies tap us on the shoulder
to remind us that we are animal
and there is still something that stirs us
enough to want to be of this world.

## It's a Dandelion

What is ugliness? What fails to please? I've started to wonder about this. It surprises me that I haven't wondered about this until now, until this age of myself. But, really, what is it and who says that it is? A woman with curves? A woman without curves? Symmetry? Asymmetry? The creek when it is low? The creek when it is high? Something dark? I'm trying to recall if I've ever heard something light called ugly. It's troubling me.

So, then, beauty is readily agreeable? Actually, not. This planet hosts so many worlds, how will we ever find each other by the billions? Maybe it will take the newborns and the wisdomed. There is more agreement at the beginning and when we near the end. Try to find middle ground. Oh, yes, that's it: what is hallowed and what is not. May there always be spirit in my matter, and yours. And, that plant – do you know it? It's a dandelion. But still, you should ask its name and what you are good for to it. Maybe it will consider you. Maybe it will cock its bright yellow head your way, look up, and decide.

## Madre de la Selva

You lure and captive-ate me
in your viney, gemstone
tendrils
like a love note or a thorn,
sent from afar, deeply penetrating
   – me and time –
anonymous and humid.

Blood courses, flows, beads, spills.

What ancient longing stirs,
haunts,
indigenous, naked, and savage,
recollecting in
cellular memory
Life
herself –
birthed the writhing, suckling, murderous
Goddess of Fertility
and Death,
encoupled,
serpentine,
and staring me in the I?

Ah! Bless the inner knowing –
a sensuous passage
awaits,
emergence from your
purgatorial embrace,
and after glow.

# The Blue Iris

But, what if it is the blue iris?
What if that is all we need to speak
to God, or the gods, or some other
form of the sacred?

I try to pay attention. I piece words together.
This is prayer, yes. But, more so, it is ceremony.
I want to hear another voice. I want a reply.
I want to know that I'm not alone and that
all of this matters.

May I put it in a vase?  May I decorate my home
with it? It is beautiful.

Could I be worthy of something
that I love?

## The Crocus

You haven't been able to see it, but it has been there all along. There, in the darkness. The harsh times always ask us to put faith in the invisible.

I've watched the gaunt squirrels searching for it. Sometimes they prevail, pressing their noses into leaf litter and mulch. Scratching. Sniffing again. Scratching some more. Then, they get greedy.

Often, they move on, sad and empty, but hopeful that something else will satiate. Soon. And, it continues to be there, contemplating its worth and waiting to be of some beautiful use.

I wonder what goes on inside of it when the Earth's embrace turns from hard and cold to soft and warm. Surprise? Delight? A teary emotional release?

Something like that, I imagine.

By this age, you'd think I'd know. For sure. But I don't. I will tell you

when I do.

# The Dogwood

Today
on the mountain
I walk between the veils,
pondering neither here
nor there and what it means
to not know what a future holds.
The trees offered me boughs of
white flowers, petals not yet
fully unfurled, like butterfly wings
not yet dry and ready for escort.
There was something
about the mists that held memories
and promises in the nothingness.
But I kept coming back to the flowers,
something about something I had
read long ago about something
of Christ they were said to symbolize.
Something. I can't remember,
not that it would matter much
anyway; I don't need old stories
to define truth and beauty for me.
I can know it for myself, here
in these mountains, here
on this branch, here in this body
where my heart is open and wide
like a blossom ready
to be picked by someone
for someone special.

## The Garden Iris

In the florescence of the garden iris,
I see your green eyes
when bright and when wearied
by days grown frail in their
failure to keep on making promises
about tomorrow.

You just rest now.

Let what has already bloomed be enough.

Someone will remember it next spring,
and perhaps the one thereafter.

Love has a way of rising when tears
water the soft mossy earth.

I'll plant memories for you with my own
body while answering the question,

"What is it the Soul wants to live into?"

Because I learned from you

what a life can be.

# The Last Day

I hope the last day of the world comes in the springtime when everything is beautiful and promising new beginnings. I would be happy and planting seeds in the garden and dreaming of the orchard's juicy fruit offerings not far off and I wouldn't be wanting for much besides sunshine and long days and, well, nights warm enough for star gazing. I love the heavenly stories of old. If I knew of it, I'd be urging everything into loveliness. Death can come when it comes but before then there is the droning of bees in sweet-scented meadows and the shapeshifting of cloud animals ambling mountain ridgetops and a frog or two upon the lilies croaking and twanging and I'll have a need to kiss them. When the sun slides away for the last, you won't find me fretting. All of this came out of darkness. All of this will come out of darkness again – though we won't remember it – it will all be so miraculous.

# The Redbud (Pleasure)

The redbud, that spring exclamation, that evidence that this wise world invented flowers. It put them on trees. Look up! That color! Pink doesn't permit the sullen. Here come the bees out of the old locust. That buzzing! They're shaking the pollen loose. Isn't this delightful? Isn't this exciting? Isn't this what it's like to wake in the mountains just as the new light falls upon the old patchwork quilt? Isn't this what it's like to be content with your decisions, maybe even pleased? The redbud!

# The Rhododendron

*Rhododendron* from the Latin rhododendron,

rose-tree.

An evergreen shrub.

☙

In spring, nearing summer, when light breezes run
mountain slopes, a rhododendron found me upon the
woodland trail, blooming wide, open and earnest.
Did my presence please the plant and place?
Petals, pink-rimmed, at my feet as if I were
the one to be adored. Heavenly the moment
and the thought of it, beauty and devotion,
as if I were suddenly inhabiting one of the stories
told of the old masters. What borrowed bliss!
But borrowed it is, like claiming the delight
manifest of a peacock's spread as my own
capacity to charm.

The Rhododendron!

There is wisdom in this folly.
This is a game of seeing and being seen,
of good cheer and optimism that beauty still
has willing witnesses and those who wish
to be known by it. Why waste love on conditions?
Compassion does ignorance in every time.
How steadfast the duty of the flower that lined
the temple steps to grow where heathens roam freely.

Always it is in the wild that the winds of change
loose us of one thing to make way for another.
Nature expresses her fondness through
the exuberant flower and floralled floor equally.
Of Emerson too, it was Rhodora who beguiled.

Do not tell the rose.

# The Unfurling

I cannot help but be moved
by the silent unfurling
of fiddlehead and
floral opulence.

What if I could come undone
with such beauty
and willful surrender?

Grace is the heart throb of the Beloved.

Let me speak with a tongue
of liquid pearls
and repeatedly turn myself
inside out
until my heart is evident to even
the weariest eye.

This, I feel,
is what it means
to unfold –
to risk to blossom
amidst a world of witnesses.

## The Way a Flower Opens

Have you ever been kissed the way
a flower opens? Those with short lives
must know something of pleasure,
mustn't they? And beauty, whether
it be their own or they just choose
to find it everywhere. I think that
flowers must kiss bees, and butterflies,
and, yes, the heavenly air as much as
they dare. I won't say an unkind thing
about that.

# The Fiddlehead Song

The voice rose like musty fragrance,
from leaf-littered substrate to my ear.

"Do you love me?"

I stooped low.

"Do you love me?"
inquired harlequin green fern
in fiddlehead curl and tuck.

"Of course I do,"
I replied.

"Then, please sing me a song."

I balked.

Here the delicate melodings of thrushes
disarm choirs of angels
hand-selected by the gods.

I could offer nothing better than an
off-pitched Corvid grok.
On a good day.

"I can gift you some water,
or how about my favorite ring?"

I was hopeful.

"Sing me a song."

My hopes were dashed.

So I sat there at trailside for 36 straight hours,
nervously relocating last autumn's acorns among piles.

How to honor, not insult?

I mused and agonized
as sunlight and moonlight
took turns wandering through the nascent woods.

And then a cool breeze stirred
the understory and me.

"It's all about intent,"
came the re-minder from my
exasperated mystic pal
on a higher mountain far away.

"Intento!"

Indeed.

I sighed and giggled at
my human folly.

And then I claimed
who I am.

Fire ignited deep within my belly cauldron,
causing feisty cleansing steams
to rise within
and purify.

Dews burning off at dawn
serve the forest similarly,
perhaps.

And so, with great intent, I sang:

"I love you…"

to the harlequin fiddlehead,

alas,

my voice every bit as
unabashedly wretched as I'd feared.

Alas.

But before I could offer up an apology
worthy of such outlandish disgrace,

the *Osmundia* fern replied:

"That's the most beautiful
thing I've ever heard,"

and unfurled.

# What We Want from a Flower

Tell me nothing,
and I won't believe
you. Within you
there is longing,
something

that you want from
a flower, maybe it
isn't a fancy thing,
but I'll bet it is
profound. Life

changing, maybe.
Have you thought
about this? I hadn't
until today. I'm

thinking about
it now, how I want,
no, expect, flowers
to make things
better. They do. Isn't

this interesting? I wonder
what a flower wants,
no, expects, from
me.

# Summer

# A Hot Summer

A coneflower boldens the meadow.
A patch of scarlet beebalm nectars a hummer.
Ephemerals melt away in unnoticed silence,
        what happened to last month's admiration?

The tall grasses host bright green hoppers and mantids,
Attract the does. This is where they nestle their fawns.
Bears and coyotes figure it out.

The sun has much to say this year – hot stones, fire-brand air.
Road dust rises in thick clay clouds, chokes roadside vegetation,
Plants breathe, until they can't,
    imagine the droughted struggle they endure auto after auto –
I want the plants to sing and I want to sing with them:
    "Givers of the Rain, hear our sorrow and our plea."

   Leaves yellow, brown at the edges
      crisp and fall into tindered duff,
We are all wilting. We are all wilting.
This is what it is like to have love withheld
    from the embodied soul
       wilting –

   The garden says that it cannot give
      if I will not give,
and a well that runs dry demands
      hard choices of us.

            Today, I choose to fill buckets for the goats.

How deep do the roots of the sycamore go?
And the poplars and maples and hickories?
Deep enough to quench a La Niña summer thirst?
The Storyteller Oak has looked over the old homestead
    for centuries and can speak of resilience –
        human and tree and I've heard tales
            of an old mule who grew onery with his fate
              but kept one living in his rugged hide.

Yes, there are those who can be counted on to carry on.
The goldenrod, the yucca, they seem okay with things
            for now,
                their ancestors reminding them how
                    they've done this before and learned
                        how to count on more in life than rainfall.

This could be it; I suppose –
the beginning of a grand grief for loves lost,
for change that is not of the seasons,
not a way to keep the body in Earth time.

But all that done and said,
    I still want to show up and celebrate the breath of my breath.
I want to put faith in roots that run deep,
in seeds that get carried away by wind, by bird,
    horded by the white-footed mouse.
        May they someday make the best of their separation.

I'm here to tell you that something
or someone
lives to tell about it.

# A Summer Moment

Summer resides at the confluence
of rushing to be and utter stillness.
We must bloom. We must rest.
And, at some point, there is
a moment in which blooming
and resting are indistinguishable.
Our lives have summers.

# Before Falling was a Fear

I climbed trees. Trees, many trees, invited me into their sky-reaching boughs to play – Come! – offering promises of joy and grandeur. Knees bark-burned, I – the tomboy – always said, Yes! I could be pleased high in a cedar or oak. Once I shared a dogwood with a young rat snake who flicked his tongue in and out, in and out. Neither of us was bothered by the other. I came down first. I wonder what became of him.

When you are in a tree, the deer will walk right under you and – shocked – contemplate why they are looking up at the creature that you are. Birds may say, "Oh, you've finally remembered." I think I know what they mean but it's not something I can talk about with other people. So, I don't. I do peer into nests of little beggars and feel like I remember something.

I've had people hold tall ladders for me so I could squeeze a hand into a hole in a long-leaf pine and pull-out screeching, beak-nipping, little woodpeckers. It's amazing how much a woodpecker nip to the finger hurts. Ouch! Red-cockadeds are endangered. We put numbered metal bands on their legs. Sometimes, a colored band too. There are more of them to count now than then. Still though, not enough.

I don't think I'll ever get over history lessons about trees and the sight of ropes dangling in my mind's eye. No doubt, the trees wanted nothing to do with it.

People are planting trees now – lots of trees – but not to climb, not for joy. They want the trees to save them from themselves. It's a discussion that I have yet to take up with trees. I'm curious how they feel about becoming saviors to the human species. It must be so strange for them, under the circumstances.

We lived in trees – you know - before, I suppose, falling was a fear.

# Berries

A container full of berries
is a measure of time
and effort,

and something
else that escapes the
lid and is the sweetest.
I could say more, yes,

but I want you to
find out for yourself
how summer frees

things. It can be hard
to remember.

# Berry Picking

Right arm outstretched.
Thumb and forefinger
poised for delicate
pluck.

Memory and anticipation
rise and spiral
like two strands of DNA
in a rambunctious act of creation.

Herbaceous nibbles,
red and robust,
are offered in abundance
at the sky-cast perk
of bramble tangle

not by accident.

Summer's succulence
is juicy bait for the soul.

Court it,

And eventually you'll learn
that every thorn in life
is an invitation to
slow down
and be attentive.

It's the only way
to harvest fruits.

# Bloom

If you were a flower,
would you let someone hold your petals
shut so that you could never bloom?

You are a flower…
The embodied floral essence of your soul,

And I'm imploring you,

imploring you,

Resist everything and everyone that holds back
your most glorious unfurling!

The Heavens beckon you to reveal
your untamed beauty and offer your unique gifts
through acts of intimacy with the Sacred Other.

How tender the touch of butterfly and bee…

Feel it.

Feel it upon your own skin –
that potent co-mingling of
tenderness, intent, and outcome.

What are you waiting for?

Vow to leave nothing of benefit to
this crazy world hidden.

Vow to make vulnerable what the fearful ego
most demands you protect.

Vow to scream "Yes! Yes! Yes!" to the cosmos at that
very moment you reach ecstatic heights of blossoming.

I don't care if you are in a drumming circle, mosque, or grocery
store line...

The more public the better.
Inspire others to long for your courage,
and their own experience.

Scream, "Yes!"

Saying "Yes" in your own voice,
to your own magnificent display of beauty,
is the most powerful way of saying "No"
to anyone or anything that
would seek to keep you
closed up,
closed off,
shut up or
shut down.

Let me witness your radiance –

Let us witness your radiance –

Bloom!

## Grape

When the old campesino's
sun parched fingers
pluck you,
engorged and readied
by your own sweetness,
how do you feel?

# Lavender

The bumble bees and I
are drawn to elongated
crowns of lavender flowers
on erect emerald stems.

Only in a world in which
souls can rub up against each other
could you find such creation –

enticing to all the senses.

Let me be here in the physical –

to feel,
to smell,
to see,
to hear,
to taste the knowable,
to intuit the great mystery.

Might these alluring blossoms
and these yielding insects
be evidence of our godliness,

and that every living thing
is a mated aspect
of heaven?

My body says, "yes."

# Lilies

What if we were
all lilies, the
kind that float
on dark, pungent waters?
We could be open
all day long and people
would come and praise
us for it,
and say things like:

"Oh, how lovely!"

and never throw a stone
or make ill remarks
about the frog
we host for a chat at noon.
I think it would be a
wondrous thing
if someone came along
and said:

"Oh, my!"

Just like that, wanting
to be open too.

But we are not all
pond lilies, are we?
Still, I think there is a way
that we could make do,
a way that we could at least

be like the famous painters who got
ideas from things as a way
of finding a passage back from
the edge of loneliness by looking
around and saying to themselves:
"Oh, this!"
Thinking beyond thought:
"This could be contentment."
I just wish the painters had realized
that the lilies weren't content.
Every plant blooms because
it is longing for the company
of someone or something.

## Listening to Trees

"Shhhh," quiet now, I implore you.
The trees have something to say
and I want to listen.

I want to listen and remember the language
of trees, the one we shared when we were
young and ancient. The one not influenced
by today's weather. The one that pulses
through animal skin and animal bones.

There are things that trees know
that I have forgotten. You too?
How do we lose touch with
what is most vital?

Just look at them:

how they can stay,
how they turn their wounds
into works of art,
how they are kind to each other
even when their branches tangle.

I think our humanity
depends on trees.

# Nectar

Sixty minutes awake in
the meadow
reveals the nature of things
someday pronounced discoveries
by those who have been
sleeping all the while.

When was the last time you
relished a sip of honeysuckle –
Really let the clear beads of nectar
languish on your taste buds
instructionally?

How many blues do you
know of the sky that has been
your companion
since birth?

The male cardinal, the wine berries,
and the box turtle's eye
are cadmium red,
alizarin crimson,
and lust.

How glorious to know a sedge
from a grass
and to fervently listen
to their stories
for sixty minutes

as the goats forage.

## Queen Anne's Lace

These changes are given to us so that we pay attention
to what is really important, ask questions,
and live restlessly enough to grow into something
earthy and divine.

When her smock arrives in the old fields, shuttling
back and forth in the breeze, I know to
reflect on gratitude:

Have I been inhabiting it well enough?

Summer days are numbered.

I've never been able to answer, yes,
but that's okay. Gratitude is a timeless thing.
You can cast it backwards or forwards and
live into it in any given moment.

And so, I'm thankful to be in the good
company of white flowers that rise
above the grass,

weaving the fabric of the
human soul.

# Spiderwort

It was the coattails
of spring laid out for
summer's arrival –
the spiderwort still deciding
between the forest's shade
and the meadow's place of exaltation
and possible reverence.
For me, it was as if I had
lived some life that was going
to be extinguished, but with
gusto and even gladness,
although I couldn't imagine
how that could possibly
arise and unfold. So, I was
there, among the bird song
that lasts the entirety
of the day as we creatures
track the illusion of
a wandering sun, gravity
not necessarily giving us
a frame of reference for
what is and what isn't.
But anyway, there are some things
to know and some things worth
the effort to understand in
the absence of knowing. Each of us
is that kind of mystery –
a perfect opportunity for
humility.
But the flowers, purple and elegant,
are so inviting and not so argumentative.

It is storied that Pocahontas enabled
John Smith to carry seeds to
English gardens.
I think it's interesting how adoration
often takes us away from home,
leaving us with the choice to root
again, or not.
So, what will summer bring?
Something else to be decided,
I am sure.

# The First Strawberries

Young grackle
blackbird
hanging at fence.
Fenced in.
Fenced out
by a foot
in-between post
death grip.

Bloated and flied.
A raucous struggle
to survive,
No doubt.

Leg wrenched
swollen
from socket.

It shit itself
and the fence.

What a way to die.

Another,
younger,
in an instant
at lawn mower blade
bade
for etiquette
and appearance,
severed.

Into the garden.

Strawberries,
the first of the season,
ripe and gifted.

Slugs,
the perfect
roundness of bite
through the night.

Rats,
like children,
sample each one
but consume none.

Molds and mildews,
their festivity,
such a wet spring.

Me,
stroked passionate
by their redness,
the vibrant boldness
and brashness
of flesh-tight
radiance,
suppleness.
sweetness.

The eyes are
on the fruit.

The body
is there for the tasting,
but only after
you've touched
the seed,
the Soul.

Life,
Let yourself
be taken
by surprise.

## The Flowers

We only lived in that house for a year and I was only six, but I remember things. Like Mom planted a row of flowers along the walkway to the front door. They were red and yellow and orange and shaped like rooster combs. "Cock's combs," a neighbor said. They fascinated me, how a flower could look like part of a chicken. I watched them for endless minutes, like I expected something to happen and didn't dare miss it. I knew something of magic then. Perhaps, I simply expected they'd become chickens, scratching about the yard for seed and small insects. But maybe it was something even more miraculous than that. Maybe it was some bigger knowing that had possession over me. I'd put some in a pot on the stoop of my first house. For no particular reason, I thought. And there would come the day when I'd be standing in the Amazon and meet a field full of the ancestors of Mom's flowers, as tall as I, and I'd feel an odd sense of family and want to tell someone about it, but there was no one to tell. Then a day would arrive when I'd

have my very own chickens and
while watching them strut, cluck,
and scratch, I'd remember being
a little girl watching flowers, and
realize that I was still watching them.

We shouldn't underestimate children.
They become something else.

# The Primary Drought

The water lilies
can't explain
why they lie in a crispy heap
on a bed of crackled red clay,

or where the frogs
have gone.

It's early in the season.

But when the rain stops
a silence sets in.

Those who have not
yet given up their bodies,
pray that Death is so otherwise
occupied that he doesn't notice
they still swill the firebrand air.

I walk through tinder fields
of tall chicory,
blue flowers closed off
to a nauseous sun.

Interesting isn't it,
how so many people
stop to talk about
the drought?

"Tragic," they say.

And I wonder about hearts folded
up tight against the light

and what it would take to saturate
the human spirit with a love
for this world.

Could our full presence
float flowers?

I'm open to the possibility.

Fear is a stingy master though,
and we in-habit the primary drought,
I think.

The torment of this craving landscape
is a merciless repercussion.

"Tragic," I say.

# The Trees Speak

Those who can hear the trees speak have never had a thought of loneliness. What they know is joy, and something of grief.

Trees tell amazing stories. Stories told by generations of trees. They pass them along. Wherever it is you stand now, there is a tree that knows the story of that place.

How do I know these things?

I'm crazy enough to ask. That's all that this delightful world requires of us:

to be crazy enough.

# The Fire Song

I have walked among the sage, brushing
it with my palms and wafting into my nostrils
the scent that lingers in the cup of my hands.
You don't forget this. Not the circumstances,
not the place. Explain this to me.

I've never seen a sage grouse dance. I've
heard tell that it's like watching a feathered
dervish making his way between the worlds.
A spiral up. A spiral down. I believe that's possible.

When I was a little girl, I'd sing a nursery rhyme
to ladybugs. Do you know it?

"Ladybug, ladybug fly away home. Your
house is on fire..."

People thought I did it because I like ladybugs,
and I do. But that wasn't it.

Have you stopped to wonder why certain plants
will come all the way across the world to ask
you what you love?

That was it.

That moment when a ladybug must stop
everything she is doing to save her home,
to save her children.

Will she?

"Ladybug, ladybug."

Do you care enough to go home?

If you listen closely, you can hear those weeds
out there singing the same song, the fire crackling.

"The sage?" They ask.

"The sage-grouse?" They ask.

So often, I've found answers to adult conversations
in the memories of my childhood.

"What do you care enough about to stop everything for?"

"The sage?" They ask.

"The sage-grouse?" They ask.

There have been a lot of fires recently.

"The sage?" They ask.

"The sage-grouse?" They ask.

Large areas going up in smoke.

How many of us remember that this is our home?
How many of us will remember that this is our home?
I love the sagebrush and the sage-grouse. I want to dwell on

the scent of sage again. I want to see that dance. I want to be close enough for dust disturbed by bird feet to settle on my boots and jeans.

I hear the song of the fire.

I want to go home.

# When Men Sell Their Souls

"When men sell their souls,
where do the souls go?"

It's an important question,
if we want to get them back.

And we should, you know.
There are good reasons to do it.

I have a deep fondness for hollow
trees, they welcome so much to live
within them: a screech owl whom I
have known personally and, on my
farm, there is an old black locust filled
with thick honeycomb and sweet,
golden honey and so many bees that
the tree hums and vibrates under a
many-lined palm laid gently upon the
vertical running bark. We keep each
other secret.

But, hollow people, they don't let
the lovely things in.

I find myself spending more and more
time with trees.

# Autumn

# Acorns

Within an acorn resides an entire tree.

Imagine! How clever the gods; they perform
this act and better it, enlisting scads of forgetful squirrels
to do their autumn planting. This world is so ordinarily
miraculous. I do hope that you have noticed.

# And the Oak

I'm wondering if you've come
to understand the simplicity
of loss – those letters never
written to an old friend.

Can you imagine a life in which
everything was held on to,
in which things just kept becoming

more and more?

Would you be able to find yourself?

Words are not words unless
they are something so important
that you let them go on their way
into the world – keeping them
makes nothing possible.

And the sun with its rays.
And the ocean with the fish that go upstream.
And the oak with every one of its leaves.

Why are you fretting?
Have you defined yourself too narrowly?
Have you believed in permanence?
Tell the truth. Have you been afraid?

I'll bet there is a leaf pile,
– large and plush –
somewhere nearby,
that you can

go

jump in

to make things right again.

# Asters (Identity Matters)

When I was a wild child, I began to name my relationships in Latin: *Rana, Elaphe, Parus, Aster,* and more. Words incarnate relationship. We use words to introduce ourselves to the possibility of being known and exploring otherness. The telling of my life joys must employ these words, in spirit if not in form. So, now I must admit to you something of my aging grief: modern science has taken my dear, long-time friends from me.

I'll just say something of the asters, the star flowers, but that's only because brevity is convenient to the heart. There were hundreds and they demanded intimacy. At a minimum, you had to be so very attentive to season, soil type, stature, colors, numbers, textures, and position to demonstrate devotion. Even with that, they might not be sufficiently satisfied with your allegiance to reveal their true nature. Now, save one, they are gone; *Aster* belongs to Eurasia, replaced in the New World with ten big words that have nothing to say about the person I have become: *Almuster, Canadanthus, Doellingeria, Eucephalus, Eurybia, Ionactis, Oligoneuron, Oreostem, Sericocarpus,* and *Symphytotrichum*. Now, every time I walk down my drive or hike the country road up to the mountain top, I'm faced with a crisis of identity at the edge. Who are you? Who am I? It pains the memory of what was.

But then, there was this lovely autumn afternoon, when I approached some particularly tall, particularly beautiful flowers that had caught my attention. Before I had the chance to sigh, they said, "You can live another life, start off as a child again." And there was the permission that I didn't know I needed to belong to the world again. I was curious. She stood in a wet place, highly branching, her reddish stem holding up arms of delicate, many petalled, purple flowers. I told her my name (which I suddenly recalled is not my childhood name) and acknowledged her by who she has grown to be: *Symphytotrichum puniceaum*. She, like me, is a lover of swamps and the things that were once-upon-a-time *Rana* who dwell there.

## Asters Under a Hunter's Moon

In bold defiance of nothing
we convene under the Hunter's Moon,
white asters blooming
thighs to ankles,
a wedding train
that spans the width of this trail
and down the path
eternally.

Life proposed at conception,

but it has taken me
decades to yield to
my worthiness as a blushing bride.

The owl says, "Who?"

And I declare, "me" –

Committing to an inextricable partnership
with the world
at the altar
of a humble and privileged
embodiment.

This breath says, "Yes."

And so does this one.

# Bittersweet

The bittersweet vines hung there, in the trees,
by the dusk-cast river, orange berries bursting
from papered-sheaths.

I understood bittersweet.

You?

*

Sometimes we walk in circular paths that
make what is new seem so familiar,
sometimes, because it is.

This is our challenge: to distinguish reality
from mystery while never choosing
reality over the other.

You know what it is like when something
that lived a certain destiny becomes something
else entirely because it was loved in
a certain way.

That's the nature of all things. Or it could be.

*

When the sun set, I knew that it was still there,
on the trees, but I walked away anyway.

Bittersweet remains.

There is a dear, dear sweetness in that.

# Blue Lobelia

The blue lobelia has arisen
and opened its mouths to
the bumblebees.

These are the days to take
nothing for granted.

That droning cicada might be the last.
That creaking katydid might be the last.

The butterflies are lying, spent, on the ground.
The warblers are starting to sneak away in the night.

The squirrels are frantic.
There is no acorn mast this year.
They wonder how they will ever gather
and open enough walnuts and hickories
to make it through.

Odds are, many of them won't.
Death frightens.

Maybe I'll put out corn this winter.

Have I taken the time to search out a bird's nest and count the eggs?
Have I sat long enough among the tall meadow flowers?
Have I told the fat, rough-bodied toads how truly lovely they are?
Have I let at least one mystery take hold of me?

What will it be like when the first flurries come?

Will I look back, wondering where I had been all this time?

# Fallen

Did you notice how, when the oak leaf fell – dead, dry, and umber – it chose beauty as its resting place? It chose fractals of afternoon light. It chose colors bold and vibrant, yet tender. It chose waters gently talking their way into the winter months, and the months beyond.

When angels fall is there grace in the descent? You've seen those mysterious soft-white feathers slowly swinging their way to earth, haven't you? And you stopped everything to look up in wonderment, didn't you? So then, the answer is yes, isn't it?

When the nuts fall – walnuts, hickories, hazels – and the acorns – thick or long-bodied – and the fruits – whether berries or those dear sweet persimmons and pawpaws – something beautiful always arrives and arises. Life goes on like this, doesn't it?

I've fallen. There have been scrapes, bruises, breaks, and stitches. They have been literal. I cried. They have been metaphoric. I screamed. Those are the biggest ones, the hardest ones. The most painful and scarring.

No one ever told me that it is possible to fall beautifully.

I'm learning to do that now.

There is a leaf in a stream.

# Ginseng Thieves

I found them on knee, on a Saturday morning,
digging three-pronged ginseng.

I told them to stop. And go. And was
only semi-polite about it.

They seemed surprised that I could arrive
there, just then, and spot
them in their leafy camo, such baggy pants,

and that I could speak a thing or two about the blond
roots (they'd broken most of the root hairs) gripped in
their pocket-buried hands, to which
red clay still clung, hopeful, that I'd get it set back
within this Earth;

It still had work to do:

this world needs holding.

※

This is what it is like to suddenly
realize that you are inhabiting
your belonging:

The forest had called out
to me by a name

I knew.

# Goldfinches on Sunflower

Someone planted sunflowers,
likely a great big field, lovely,
like the one in my imagination,
collected seed, and sent to
someone who put it in artful little
envelopes. Then, someone shipped
those envelopes to a store where
someone put them in a bountiful display.
I saw it there, wandered over, and made
my selection: sunflowers. Someone took
my money at the cash register. Well, truth
be told, I used a credit card. I drove home.
I waited until the ground warmed enough.
That took earnest weeks of patience.
Then, hooray, I ripped open the envelope,
dove my long fingers in, picked out white-
and-black-striped seeds and plopped them
and prayers, one at a time, into the small
holes I'd made along the fence line, at the
edge of the garden. I waited and watched.
I watched and waited as they grew. Tall,
taller than me, with big golden heads,
weighted ever more with thick rows of seed
that followed the mathematical principles
of sacred geometry. That fascinates me.
It was late summer when the goldfinch
arrived. It took a lot of us and a lot
of work to make that moment.

# Leaving

On these mornings you can hear the trees themselves speaking, not the birds that have lifted into currents and gone on two miraculous wings. There is grief in their voices, and relief. You know what this feels like if you have lived. Leaving: letting go of what no longer serves the body and soul, often the heart. I can stand by, beside and underneath, and give some sense of comfort by telling them how beautiful this process is, how I admire the way they do it with the bold prospect of witnesses.

I think that relating to the leaf is harder than relating to the tree, unless you consider that the bird left the tree for some grand adventure, and then you go on to realize that we are all leaving each other constantly.

Our old selves, too.

It was a tree, on one of these delicate barren mornings, that said to me: "I love to watch you change and grow."

# Pawpaws

Me, down by the river.
The pawpaws, down by the river.
The crickets rubbing autumn songs
into the cool morning air
where the woodland sunflowers
and goldenrod stand tall,
where they flank fields in which
black angus fatten.

This remembering is a lonely
remembering –
this reaching of the hand
to the green bulbous fruit,
this testing for softness
between thumb and index finger,
this joy in the hand,
this cradling of the harvest –
oblong and dense –
the anticipation of taste,
the flesh: yellow, smooth soft,
the taste itself –
like no other, though some
claim an apple custard, of sorts –
and the seeds,
the dark, thick, smooth seeds
and the promise they make,
if you treat them just right.

There had been baskets
and women's stories
and laughter.

## The Annual

Your presence would
terrify me
if it weren't my desire
to be destroyed.

I am like the flower
who yearns to drop my
petals so that I may
go to seed,
and bloom anew as
an entire meadow
perfuming the sky.

This self is a limited
concept –

it pushes hard against
my inner skin,
saying,
"Let me out!"

The tight-bodied seed
of me cracks open.

The unfurling sprout of me
rises through the soil,
wishing to speak only
in the plural.

This is how I live –
rooted and
reaching for the sun.

And this is why
I choose to die
an annual –

So that there is more
of me to give of myself
to you.

# The Cattail

"I thought that I had told you
about joy," said the cattail…

Toes wiggling in the soft
marsh muck,

Practiced hips swaying
in the breeze,

Undressing silky seed tufts
with a pleasurable sigh
and impish grin.

"Were you not listening?"

# The Names of Trees

I don't know the names of the trees under which the names of my bloodlines were born. It's been hundreds of years since they were sung into the ears of the newborns as a welcoming. There is no one left to ask of these things. No one. I'll attest there are some hints in the woods of the antiques that came, crated with hopes and dreams, on last-earnings-spent ships but, even then, not so much as there have been rough passages. I think about the courting that took place to get me here: under what shade were lovely things whispered and innocence lost, into what bark were initials carved, what gave of itself for the sweet-scented nosegays, what fed the hearth fires? It's a thing to have forgotten! Once the crest, once the clan, once the heart of the land that nourished the belly and the spirit. Once where prayers were hung and gods made their capricious intents known. Who are we absent the trees? How have the trees fared in our long absence? I wonder. I think I shall ask the trees in the neighboring woodland to tell me the names of all those they are missing.

## Then, Nothing

I try to believe in change as a trustworthy passage
Seeing how floral and leaf make their way,
Giving themselves over to formlessness
day by day releasing evermore from living
Exuberance; here and gone before we know it,
Permanence our hallucinogenic tonic
Certainty the addiction.
I have a desire:
I want to become one who reaches for the sun.
I want to become one who roots deeply in the earth.
Then, nothing.

# Th Wedding Flower

It was in the road, fallen, unable
to attend the wedding that was in progress
when I was hiking up the mountain and
came across it. It was orange because
it was October. It was one of those
flowers that you buy at a craft store.
It could have ended up in a plastic
vase in a cemetery among fallen leaves,
or on a little girl's Halloween costume,
or tucked into a grapevine wreath hung
on the door to welcome guests at
Thanksgiving. But it ended up in the gravel
while vows of faith and obedience were
being made. Without a purpose
and in the dust, you could declare
it garbage and discard it without care.
But I think it knew its way. A poet
walks here routinely. Certainly, she
would see it at her feet and be able to hear
it remark how grateful it was to be in
just the right place at just the right time
to be noticed so that its story
could be told.

## To Tell the Truth About Persimmons

I have welcomed
the frost
that ends
the summer

and reached
high into the branches
plucking
softened fruit

Believe me
the wait was worthy
this tartness
this earthiness
this reason to live a life

# Until, Then

I can't imagine the lovely flowers want an ending
after so much attentiveness from the bees
and passersby.

Is there grief when the first petals fall away?
I feel some, certainly.

The exuberant summer is relinquished
for seasons of humility.

But still there is the goldenrod for company
And the golden spider upon its web
And I shall be pleased by this suspension of time
until the winter wren takes to the sumac,
flakes of snow in the air.

# When Dreams Dry Up

There are dreams,
like fruits,
which pucker and shrivel
on the stem.

The erotic drip of juice from your chin
is not guaranteed,
no matter how intimate
your relationship
with tree,
and blossom,
and pollinator.

I looked upon such a dream-fruit
today.

There was grief,
and that old familiar smell
of truncated memories.

I had a mind, for a moment, to pluck
the shrunken, hard dried mass
and take it into ceremony,

but my hand stopped,
suspended,
in mid notion.

Aghast.

What arrogance to think that any
intervention on my part would grant
a more holy passage
than destiny's plunk into the cradle
of leaf and microbes!

And that's what I learned today
about dreams –

Sometimes, part way is fruition.

Sometimes,
it's best to simply step back
and let the energies
return to their source for re-cycling.

So, to the being on the stem,
I bowed in prayer position
instead.

# WINTER

# Below the Crisp-Capped Snow

Below the crisp-capped snow,
Below the frozen duff and clay,
Sleeping seeds in their coats,
Knowing nothing of their fate,
Like when we too were preparing.
Down from the skeletal trees
Squirrels scuttle and fury-dig,
Food must be found across
The whole of the long winter.
Seeds suffice a belly's screams,
Thin the woodland necessarily,
Move the woodland necessarily
When that seed is lost to memory
Someplace else;
Hunger guides worlds into being.
What have you been missing
When hidden away?
You are animal too,
These days are meant to feed
your hunger too!
There, look upon the pine,
Strong and green and needled,
Listen to its winter words,
No whispering from its boughs!
Do you know what you are searching for?
Do you know what is searching for you?

# Fallow

Plowed and harrowed,
but left unseeded.

What an odd and exhausting
period of rejuvenation
this is.

The dark rich soil of me longs
to support new growth,
to feed Life-sustaining nourishment
to a soul-starved world.

Oh please,

Tell me what nutrients
I still need claim
to be deemed worthy of seed.

Kernels of hope fly past
in crow beaks
but there is never an
effort made to plant.

Rain comes,
and the sun shines
deliciously upon my hungry body
but I have nothing
to bequest in reciprocity.

So deeply rooted
are my woes
amidst this positively-intended
abandonment.

I wonder in the dark hours,

Is it the chemistry of tears
you seek?

And I offer electrolyte salts
in streams.

Still I remain fallow.

Hafiz tells me
a divine seed, the crown of destiny,
is hidden and sown on an ancient, fertile plain
that I hold the title to.

How then does one reveal the
fore-ordained gift of self?

Dowsing with willow brings
me to the core:

Embryo and endosperm.

In essence, it is me
feeding the offering
of sustenance that
is myself.

I am entitled to give.

These sweet tears of joy
 I absorb,
and swell.

And swell.

So this is what it feels like
to break free
from the hardness
and rise!

# In the Belly

In the belly places, what was seeded grows,
readying for emergence:

What was never before, will be.

A beginning has been planning itself
out of everything that has been lost to you.
What is to become of it already knows your dreams,
has been witness to your darkest moments –
the spinning, the turning, you've been going
through to get into just the right position.

But you are still anticipatory.

Growth is not the delivery process.
It is what promises delivery.
Something more is needed for a departure
from that which restricts:

>  An opening.
>  Suffering.
>  Severance.
>  Anonymity.

>  A claiming.

Comfort's promises are meaningless then,
lest anything become familiar and creation
be stifled in its grand play.
Where turmoil and whimsy are indistinguishable,
the threshold is to be found. Something there knows

just how to call upon your vulnerabilities
until it has you screaming, "No more!"
because you are no longer willing to be
that life, in that way.

You're willing to bargain away your name.

What your soul longs for awaits beyond the misery
of the breakthrough and fall,
the forcing gasp that fills tender lungs with new air,
the light entering opened eyes and the instability
on new ground –
wherever it is that desire will have taken you to.
It's a destination and it is not. Rest only briefly
in your bewilderment –
You won't be able to stay here. Cut the cord.
Beginnings aren't the path and they too
must be left behind, forgotten, not even
to be reserved as fodder for your own storytelling.
Declare yourself and then get on with it.
Let risk bring you to your senses and rewards.
Let there be reason in your magnificence.
Let gratitude infuse your being,

until the seasons turn once more.

# Leaves Rising

Each winter there's a moment
in which my lungs are
completely freed
of stale air –

The daffodils are rising!

"Oh!"

This, I think, is what it is
to acknowledge prayers
answered:

To fall to one's knees.

Just like this.

This is what it is to voluntarily
enlist as the voice of an
encouraging angel
for little, faithful plants who
have been tucked away
in the cold and dark
of the underworld,

Somewhat forgotten.

I reach out and stroke
the green, sleek, blade-like leaves,

So bold against the
dank rot
and gray.

Oh, yes.

I shall push through,
again.

## One Winter

I loved a place where the trees and I knew each other by name, where they had begun to reclaim what the soldiers and homesteaders had cleared to make way for life-death struggles in the name of freedom. I helped them as best I could, freeing them of entanglements with marauders and returning those lost from place. In the damp of autumn, soft-bodied mushrooms pushed their way up and into my grateful hands. In the spring, the ephemerals saved me, year after year. There were squirrels dedicated to the walnut grove, deer cheek-thick with acorns, more berries than the birds could steal away despite my eager generosity. I left it one winter, foolishly believing in the very same dreamscape that had been marketed to those the soldiers and homesteaders. Again, promises were broken. Displacement: I believe our grief is the land's grief. We are both bought and sold, both made to disappear, both sick with the longing to be unowned. There is no homecoming as long as there is othering. Human. Humus. The rest of my days are dedicated to restoration. I want to find my way back to the place that is every place, where my name is indistinguishable from the landscape of the living and the disposed of form, where love makes it impossible to separate us again.

# Plants in Winter in Six Verses

**1.**

For me, winter is a haunted time. The cold awakens memories in my bones. Harshness. Scarcity. Loss. Loss of whom or what I do not know, but it's meaningful – to someone, it was meaningful, so meaningful that the old sorrow has not yet left this world for the next. It arrives on the dusk of short days, stands at the woodland edge, and waits.

**2.**

I love the hollies. Evergreen and red berries. They tell you if the deer have come to nibble when the flurries change the world. See the spines on the leaves? This is telltale, but not sufficient if the snows challenge the scraping of cloven hooves, snow remaining deep and crusted, denying. But for the birds, there is welcoming: "Come! Come!" And they do, though often late in the season after responding to the more pleasing invitations. They come: robins of red breast, famished flocks of waxwings, the mockingbird when silent long enough to nab and swallow. Sometimes the cardinal, maybe the jay. When the boughs are stripped of crimson, shat seeds become a forest's hope and dreams.

**3.**

I remember one winter holiday when a sprig of mistletoe was hung from the mid-century chandelier, in the foyer, two steps across the threshold. No one let the spell be cast upon them. Pity, that.

**4.**

When my parents divorced, making do meant we'd do without a Christmas tree. My sister wailed. My mother grabbed an old, dull handsaw and took to the scant woods behind our home. She cut down short, spindly cedars – two – stripped the bows from one and staple gunned them onto the narrow spine of the other. "It's a Charlie Brown Christmas!" she said, proudly. My sister kept all her friends away.

5.

The Yule log laid out in the Great Hall. The licking of flames. Heat pushing the cold air back just so far. A gathering of celebratory souls eager to cast wishes and blessings into the fire upon the body of holly sprigs. This was ceremony. I wondered if they wondered about the grand familiarity of it all. How does the forgotten find its way to us again?

Maybe they were just having fun. Maybe I was the only one who could still smell the wassail, spiced and ready to warm a soul.

6.

Praise the lengthening days, the removal of layers, and everything that saves us. The first crocus warms the spirit beyond measure. Purple, bold, defiant. How I love it and love myself again.

# Pruning

Can you live with the scent
of larkspur on your lips
while others seek to destroy you
because of memories
they can't recall?

Truth is not found on the
material plane.
It resides in the imprints
you've left during your
comings and goings
on the other side.

Don't let yourself be hooked
into playing a role you
died to lifetimes ago.

The Beloved never manifests
a single rose.
You too must choose to
be a bloom a hundred times over.
Let the thorns be protectors
not villains.

And even if the shears do come,
bless your courage
for having shown up in this life
well enough
to be noticed.

## Roses Are Out of Season

Sometimes the Beloved
is a place
that chooses you
in your sleep
while you are busily dreaming
of a human form that hasn't yet
crossed the threshold of your
weary front door.

How bittersweet the sip of tonic
when you realize that
the reclining land on which
you've been walking barefoot,
while casting your laments like seed, has
been – all the while – caressing your
filthy, calloused feet,

that the dawns that you casually inhale
with your first morning breath have been
the red lips of the horizon

starting your day with a wide-reaching kiss, and

that the feeling of being unable to move,
what you've fought like a panicked person
in a pool of quickening sand,
was really the sensation of being held in a
long, conditionless embrace.

I've seen this: how some people
can't get away – how they eventually
surrender in love, or misery.

The one who calls you home
has many faces,

Today, I recognize him in yellowed
walnut leaves
falling on the path ahead of me.

Roses are out of season.

## The Ancestral Tree

What is the name born of my ancestral tree?
Oak, yew, species extinct and nameless –
How does it move in the storm winds?
Bending, twisting, breaking –
I believe there is a knowing: how and why we abandoned
its sheltering arms where lovely birds once chorused –
I believe I can still hear the anguished cries of the felled
and split and also the bereavement of dry leaves refusing to release
themselves to the duff, hanging on over the very long, cold winter –

I wear the bark of this lineage: thick, tough, rough to the touch.
Too, I am a woman who plants trees in rich compost in holes
I've labored into red clay starved and stripped of good relations.
There is no end to the task, this right, this ritual –
Reconciliation is a forest in the making.

I cannot know the unknowable –
I can make a place for birds to perch above my grave –
Have you heard that singing urges growth, urges beauty?
I wish I had been taught the song of my people.

Setting seed is an act of vow making. All vows must be tended.
Along the river, at field edge, where the line ends on the mountain,
the others are making vows too –
Listen, if you can hear the trees talking.
Listen, if you can't hear the trees talking.

There is sun. There is rain.
There is the possibility that the trees will dance again
come the winds of change.

## The Berries

I could have picked
them. I didn't. Red.
Round. Winter saying
something, boldly.
Maybe to the red
bird in the green-
boughed pine. Maybe
to me. But I have a
thought. It's about
beauty. Maybe it's a
test. The important
kind. Maybe someone
up there wants to
know if you can see
a thing and praise it
and that is all. This
I've tried. I can't do
it. Every time I walk
away, my heart is
full.

# The Black Walnut

When I arrived here things
were not as I had expected,
not at all, truth be told.
On my first night, I slept
out on the deck, under the
stars and the arm of a tree.
In the night, she came to me,
a bright shining she who
was the tree and she said,
"I know why you are here. The
land called you here." With
that, she left, but I did not.
One day, a man came up the
drive in an old rust-bottomed
pick up. He thought me a fool.
"Mam, I see ya got these big
ol' trees, dangerous, gonna fall
on yur place. I'll cut 'em fer ya,
even carry 'em away, cheap."
I know a thing or two about
being swindled, and also how
to talk like I'm from a place.
"Sir, ain't nobody gonna touch
my black walnuts! Not today,
not ever. No, Sir, they ain't.
Now, git!" He understood me.
The truck bumped its way back
down the drive at, quite remarkably,
twice the speed it had arrived.
He hasn't called on me since.
So, the black walnut grove still

extends its arms, still embraces
my little cabin, still embraces me,
still knows secrets that
I haven't yet learned
of myself.

# The Roots

There's a little boy that I've been
watching,
all dressed in white linen,
on his knees,
digging,
desperately seeking the roots.

He's finally found them,
fingers raw and blooded by
perseverance,
but there they are –

long residing at the base of
Rumi's lamenting reed.

Cut off from our ancient lineage
we cannot but cry out
for a vision of Home –

though the meaning of the
deep inner wailing may
elude us for many generations,

and the masks we take up
make us unrecognizable even
in our own mirrors,

we cannot deny the sound
emanating from our own
severed soul.

It's the one that constantly
tells us that we don't belong here,

that we have been forsaken,

and that we have forsook.

Rumi's reed longed for a heart
so that it could explain
the pain of its yearning
to return to its roots.

This I have.

And so let me tell you how
I have ached:

Like the fledgling thrown
from the nest,
thinking its tending parents
now want it destroyed
on the hard ground below.

Like the autumn leaves
torn away by winds before
they had conversed
long enough to learn the
names of all the other leaves
on all the other branches.

Like the rock rolled down
the mountain slope

in the wash of heavy winter rains,
never again to know the
boulder in which it was
brought forth from the belly well
of the inner Earth.

This is the power of Love,
I am told:

To dare to risk your offspring
so that they may learn to fly.

To make offerings of yourself
to the Holy that nourishes
you from above and below.

To surrender to the pull of gravity
as a humble act of coming
onto the knees of all Creation.

To dig until the melancholy fingers yield
the droplets of bloodlines
that have departed across entire
oceans of destiny.

I am the last.

The last child has been taken
from me by the jealous hunters,
and so it stops with me.

I am the last.

I am the last to be the cut reed
and the reed cutter,

The oppressed
and the oppressor.

I am the last to forsake
the Truth
and be forsaken by
the story my lineage
construed to keep us
women safe.

Now is the time that
we must return to our
power,

That we must reclaim
the connection to our Earth-deep
roots and grow forth
again with a ripeness
that when savored
seeks only to unite.

But how?

Acknowledgment.

Acknowledging the suffering
of every reed cut
and of every reed cutter
who has been chased by
the fear of his own death.

Honoring.

Honoring the fleshy sacrifice of the reed
and the soul loss of the
reed cutter,

and the gift of shelter that they
somehow managed to
co-creatively manifest.

Learning.

Learning to hear the reed's
cry in my own voice,
and yours,
and too in the voice of the
reed cutters within.

Learning that the sound
most needed now is one
of joy.

Re-membering.

Re-membering how to find
the way back to the Earth
through dark passageways,
carrying with me every
incense-infused gift
that my ancestors have passed down
in the wrappings of the prayers that
someday,

this day,
I would take up
the alchemical bundle
called Love
and return with it to my roots.

And so I anoint that little boy
and his Mother
with the purest essence of belonging,
praying that they will no longer
feel disconnected, lonely, and unloved.

And down the matrilineal line
this too I receive.

The hungry ghosts will find that there
is nothing left here on which
to feed;

I can again draw nourishment
from who I am.

I am the black bird with a heart
who remembers the holy song
of the forgiving flute
made out of sacred reed.

## The Winter Woods

Go on thinking that this world is
barren. If you must. I shall walk
alone in the winter woods and
wonder at the stark beauty that
somehow – how does it keep
so great a vow? – manages to
remain, steadfast, in all of us.

## The Seed

If I am the embryo of the seed,
let me call this in which I am planted
my Mother's womb.

Here I am held.
Here I am nourished.
Here I am the possible human.

My umbilical chord is my root structure –
anchoring me to ancestral knowledge
and into the rich, organic detritus
of eroded lives
and savory fecal matter.

Everything that once was is a resource.

Everything.

Rain – the joy and grief of the world –
soaks and softens me.
Without it I become hardened, and
have no hope of intimacy with the light.

I must be cracked open to grow.

My limbs are the structures through which
my soul can reach, extending itself,
simultaneously longing to receive
and lamenting the ephemeral nature
of my gifts.

I show up because it's how I pray.
I unfurl because it's how I answer prayers.
I grow branches and leaves so that we have a place to meet.

I can bear flowers and fruit,
delicate, fragrant, and aphrodisiac sweet,
but not without having known relationship.

This is a place of co-creation.
Only the lonely believe in solitary forces
and the adversarial stance of their own mid-day shadow.

So, you see, these seeds of myself
that I place in your hands…

These are my way of saying, "I believe in you."

I'm asking you to do the next planting.

# White Pines

My little cabin is in what they call a holler. Here, the sun is slower to arrive than on the ridges. I prefer to meet it there rather than wait on the world's turning. Greeting the day is ritual. No, it is more than that, it is ceremony. The trees know this too, and I think also all those shrubs beneath them and the vines that use them to reach up to the heavens. Like me, climbing these mountains.

Often, the deer watch me, branches as masks. Today, it was a young white pine the doe chose. She didn't know that I knew the fawn was beside her, low in the dry stream bed, but I did. They walked on together and I, alone. What do I make of the rabbits in the grassy meadows? How are there so many, so complacent? Isn't this fox-certainty, coyote-certainty wonderful in the way that it teaches gratitude for clover and love of a moment?

Back to the white pine. There aren't many here. Not tall. Not dense. Mostly, they are young and spindly. It's like the artist had forgotten them and then suddenly said, "Oh, pines! There must be pines." Then he – or she – fit them into the remaining spaces because they are deserving. Five long needles each, that's how I know they are white pines. Of course, there are also the memories of buying them – white pines – for the dozen Christmases we were something called a family.

Once – well more than once – I sat with glorious children on a far-away mountain watching the sunset and the stars arrive, confident and twinkling. We counted them in three languages and sang songs that these same stars had taught their ancestors out of necessity. I don't remember the words, but I remember the laughter and how the night sky was caught up in their eyes. They didn't know darkness like I know darkness. I prayed they never would.

A walk isn't finished until the walker has acknowledged at least one great vulnerability and discovered something to be grateful for. I'm not talking about the pines. I am saying that maybe we should be more like artists, rabbits, and our ancestors' children.

# Winterberry

Her generosity sets in just as the sun becomes limited in his givings. "Beauty can persist through seasons of scarcity," she says. I've been learning to listen to this voice, learning to see what is ever-present. Memories can be explored in this way. Sometimes, that changes things.

## Winter Branches

Stark and haunting, yet somehow comforting on the crispest of winter days. Trees dormant yet reaching. Too late to grasp what has fallen away. Too soon to take hold of what has yet to arrive. Yet, reaching. To be so extended is the bravest of unrest, isn't it? Hundreds of millions of years of risk taking.

# Wonderland

The cold is reaching into me,
The wind blowing so very harshly;
Yet I am spellbound by wonderment
And I cannot deny the loveliness.
The greatest of trees are bowing,
Wearing a stark white shroud.
Do see how they know the holy
Is present in the thick of the storm?
The mercy of the elements is in the awe;
I could die for it in this vanishing woodland
Deeply vulnerable as I am –
Remembering these unseen forces.

# Yule

How did the holly know it would need to color gray?
And the oak, that there was good reason to hold
auburn leaves this long?
Who told them of this cold darkness and our
unadmitted need for gods to thank?
This day of this season –
when the long-nights moon gives herself over,
I know how to hear the gasp of all the living things
that have been praying for the return of the light.
What I know too, and want to say, and want you to hear
is that with the sun arises a requisite attentiveness.
What is there, right there, to see?
Can you kneel down, humbled, and act upon a thing?
Can you find yourself blessed by any revelation?
Can you remember the unuttered agreement
that holds you steadfast?
What else is there but what is before us?
Mustn't we tread this way though, now that we see it?
Now that we know?
Tell me you will greet me at dawn with joy.

# Acknowledgments

Many thanks to Mark Collins, Jason Kirkey, and Kreston Lars Johnson Scott for lending keen eyes to the draft manuscript. Your support is greatly appreciated.

Gratitude to the plants for their songs.

# About the Author

*Jamie K. Reaser, PhD,* writes at the interface of Nature and human nature. She is the author of eleven full-length poetry and lyrical prose collections, the editor of three literary anthologies, and regular contributor to literary journals. Her poetry has been commissioned for art exhibits, textbooks, biographies, and scientific publications. In addition to being an author, Jamie is a transdisciplinary conservation scientist and philosopher, nature-based soul guide, artist, photographer, and regenerative farmer. She is tended by the Rockfish River and Blue Ridge Mountains of central Virginia.

www.ingramcontent.com/pod-product-compliance
Lightning Source LLC
Chambersburg PA
CBHW030446010526
44118CB00011B/823